TALES from the TOP of the WORLD

Climbing MOUNT EVEREST with PETE ATHANS

SANDRA K. ATHANS

MILLBROOK PRESS

Morgan, Claire, Finn & Cleo –
Words and pictures on a page can stir passions and spark interests.
They can launch a very powerful chain reaction.
Take these and soar!

To Gerald, whose love and support encourage us.

To Pete, whose adventures and explorations inspire us all.

Main body text set in Univers LT Std 45 Light 9/11.
Typeface provided by Adobe Systems

Millbrook Press
A division of Lerner Publishing Group, Inc.
241 First Avenue North
Minneapolis, MN 55401 U.S.A.

Website address: www.lernerbooks.com

Library of Congress Cataloging-in-Publication Data

Athans, Sandra K., 1958–
    Tales from the top of the world : climbing Mount Everest with Pete Athans / by Sandra K. Athans.
       p.   cm.
    Includes bibliographical references and index.
    ISBN 978–0–7613–6506–8 (lib. bdg. : alk. paper)
    1. Mountaineering—Everest, Mount (China and Nepal) 2. Everest, Mount (China and Nepal)
   3. Athans, Pete, 1957– 4. Mountaineers—Biography. I. Title.
   GV199.44.E85A85 2013
   796.522095496—dc23   2011045834

Manufactured in the United States of America
1 – DP – 7/15/12

Contents

In this book, you will take a journey up Mount Everest, the tallest mountain on Earth. Your guide will be Pete Athans, a famous mountaineer. Pete has spent so much time on the mountain that he's nicknamed Mr. Everest. He has climbed Everest fourteen times and stood on top of the mountain seven times. The events you will read about are true stories from his Everest expeditions. Through his stories, you can share his

adventures and grasp firsthand what it takes to survive on Everest. You will also discover the majesty of the mountain, its beauty, and its great dangers.

Before you begin your journey, you'll need a little background on the mountain and the many people who have climbed it. Then you can take off skyward with Pete.

No Ordinary Hike

Climbing Mount Everest is no ordinary 5.5-mile (8.8-kilometer) hike. The trip from base camp to the top of the mountain can take a little over a month. Along the way, climbers might face avalanches, or masses of falling ice, snow, and rock. They might also encounter blizzards and bone-numbing cold.

Mount Everest measures 29,035 feet (8,850 meters) in height. Many climbers who try never make it to the top. They get injured, sick, or knocked down by bad weather. They must give up their dreams of reaching the "rooftop of the world."

The Many Names of Mount Everest

Mount Everest, which is located in the Asian country of Nepal, is one of many giant mountains in the Himalaya range. This chain of mountains curves across southern Asia between China and India. Local people have different names for Everest. People who live north of the mountain in Tibet (a region controlled by China) call it Chomolungma. This name means "Throne of the Mother Goddess of the Earth" in Tibetan. Nepali people, who live south of the mountain, call it Sagarmatha. The name means "Head of the Sky" in the Nepali language. In the 1800s, Great Britain controlled parts of India. In 1865 Britain named the mountain in honor of George Everest, the chief surveyor and mapmaker of the Himalayas.

Doubters and Dreamers

In 1852 British scientists determined that Everest's peak was the highest on Earth. Since then, the mountain has lured climbers from around the world. It took 101 years, fifteen expeditions, and twenty-four deaths before two climbers finally succeeded in reaching the summit (highest peak). These climbers were Edmund Hillary of New Zealand and Tenzing Norgay of Nepal. They reached the summit on May 29, 1953.

Edmund Hillary *(left)* and **Tenzing Norgay** *(right)*

Edmund Hillary took this photo of Tenzing Norgay after the pair reached the summit of Everest in 1953.

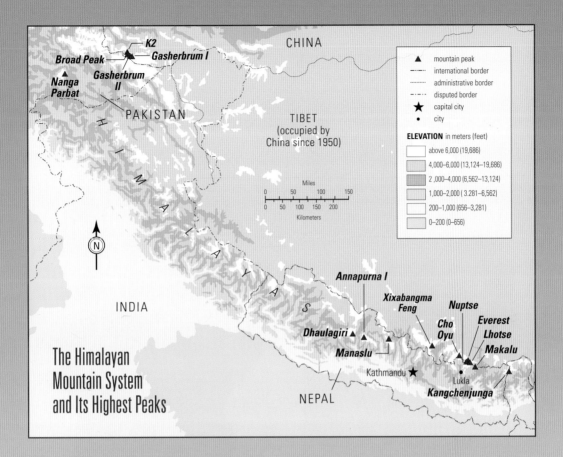

The Himalayan Mountain System and Its Highest Peaks

Who Climbs Everest?

Everest is not a mountain for beginners. Mountaineers who attempt Everest have usually scaled other peaks in the Himalayas and other high mountain chains.

Most climbers make the journey as part of an organized group. Companies sometimes sponsor, or pay for, Everest expeditions. For instance, The North Face, a company that makes outdoor equipment, has sponsored Everest expeditions to test its climbing gear. The National Geographic Society, an educational organization, has sent climbers and camera crews up Everest to make documentary films. Sometimes climbers help scientists conduct experiments on the mountain.

Some people pay money to have experienced guides lead them up Everest. But that doesn't mean just anyone can sign up and pay to go to the top. Guide organizations insist that their clients have previous mountain climbing experience. Clients must also be in top physical shape.

Most expeditions on Everest include Sherpas. The Sherpas are an ethnic group that originated in Tibet and then moved to Nepal. They practice Buddhism, a common Asian religion. Climber Tenzing Norgay was a Sherpa. Many modern Sherpas are expert mountaineers who work for mountain climbing expeditions. Sherpa staff members set up climbing ropes, carry gear to high camps, assist with medical needs and rescues, cook meals, and more.

Adjusting to Thin Air

Scientists measure the altitude, or height, of landforms by their distance above the sea (sea level). At sea level, it is easy to breathe because the air is rich in oxygen. The higher you go above sea level, the less oxygen the air holds. We say the air at high altitudes is "thin" because it has less oxygen.

At about 5,000 feet (1,524 m) above sea level, our bodies begin to sense a change in oxygen levels. People must breathe more deeply and quickly to get the oxygen they need. Above 8,000 feet (2,438 m), people can begin to suffer from high-altitude ailments. These include headaches and coughs.

A Sherpa carries a large load up Mount Everest. Thin air makes physical activity very difficult.

To keep from getting sick on Everest, climbers must acclimatize, or adjust, to the low oxygen levels. Climbers make forays, or short climbs up and down sections of the mountain, instead of trying to climb to the top all at once. Forays help climbers acclimatize to the high altitude.

Climbers Be Wary

Hold on to your balaclava! Wind gusts on Everest can exceed 250 miles (400 km) per hour. The winds come from the jet stream. This strong current of air sometimes roars across the top of the mountain. To avoid the worst of the jet stream, climbers usually tackle Everest in early May or September. At those times, the jet stream blows north of the Everest region.

On Everest, deadly snowstorms can kick up quickly, without warning. One of the worst storms ever recorded occurred in 1996. The storm engulfed the upper part of the mountain in snow. It killed eight climbers. Journalist and mountaineer Jon Krakauer described this "murderous storm" in his best-selling book *Into Thin Air*.

Altogether, bad weather has led to more than twenty deaths on Everest. Even though climbers know the dangers they might encounter, they believe the rewards of climbing Everest outweigh the risks.

A snowstorm hits a camp on Everest. Dangerous conditions can arise on the mountain at any moment without warning.

Those who dare to dream big cannot escape the lure of Mount Everest and the extreme quest to be on top . . . of the world!

—Mr. Everest

Climbers who hope to reach the top of Mount Everest begin their adventure before they even reach the mountain. They usually start in Kathmandu, the capital of Nepal. From there, they scramble aboard eighteen-passenger DHC-6 Twin Otter or Dornier 228 airplanes. Both planes are designed for short takeoffs and landings—a must when flying in the mountains.

The planes land at Tenzing-Hillary Airport in the village of Lukla, Nepal. Landings can be dangerous. The single runway is short, steep, and very busy. Slamming into the rocky mountainside, plunging into a valley, or colliding with other aircraft are real possibilities here. Pilots have no room for error on the runway.

The Trek to Base Camp

In Lukla climbers meet their Sherpa guides and porters. With the help of large, long-haired animals called yaks, porters will transport the climbers' equipment to base camp. In Lukla, at 9,383 feet (2,860 m) above sea level, some climbers suffer from a loss of breath, headaches, and coughs as their bodies try to adjust to the thin air.

Airplanes come and go from the airstrip in Lukla, Nepal.

The trek to base camp takes six to ten days. On this journey, climbers begin their acclimatization process. They might spend two nights in the same village, taking day hikes or visiting local sites. Those who climb too high too soon could get sick. They'll have to retreat to lower altitudes until they recover.

Highlights of the trek include Namche Bazaar, a bustling mountain village. From there, climbers can hike to museums, Internet cafés, a library, and Buddhist monasteries, or religious centers. Climbers can visit a bakery and taste *rigi kur*. These potato pancakes are served with yak butter. Another stop might be the village of Khunde. It is home to the area's first hospital, set up by Edmund Hillary.

Yaks transport backpacks and other luggage to the base camp on Everest.

The Seven Summits

Earth has seven continents, or giant landmasses. The tallest mountains on each of the seven continents are called the Seven Summits. Many mountaineers try to climb all seven.

NAME	LOCATION	CONTINENT	HEIGHT
Carstensz Pyramid (also called Puncak Jaya)	Indonesia	Australia/Oceania	16,023 feet (4,884 m)
Vinson Massif	Antarctica	Antarctica	16,067 feet (4,897 m)
Mount Elbrus	Russia	Europe	18,510 feet (5,642 m)
Mount Kilimanjaro	Tanzania	Africa	19,340 feet (5,895m)
Mount McKinley (also called Denali)	Alaska	North America	20,320 feet (6,194 m)
Aconcagua	Argentina	South America	22,840 feet (6,960 m)
Mount Everest	Nepal	Asia	29,035 feet (8,850 m)

Base Camp Overview

Base camp is 17,500 feet (5,334 m) above sea level. There, tents sprawl across the frosted, rocky, gray landscape. Colorful Buddhist prayer flags—emblems of peace, wisdom, and good fortune—wave in the wind. Climbers at camp burn juniper branches. This Buddhist practice is said to bring good luck. *Clank, clank, clank*—collar bells announce the arrival of yak trains. The shaggy animals lumber into camp toting supplies and equipment.

At the height of the spring climbing season, as many as five hundred people live at base camp. They include climbers from many different expedition teams. They also include day trekkers, who intend to go no higher than base camp, as well as doctors and Sherpa climbing staff. In addition, paragliders sometimes stay at base camp. These adventurers attach themselves to single-winged kites. They take off from points high on the mountain and soar like hawks on strong currents of winds.

At base camp, climbers organize gear, practice their climbing skills, and visit with others. Base camp has even less oxygen than Lukla. Climbers here might suffer from deep coughs and interrupted sleep. They might get severe headaches and lose their appetites.

Tents for climbers and guides sit beneath Buddhist prayer flags at Everest base camp.
▼

Climbers spend about two weeks at base camp. To adjust to the altitude, they make daily climbs to higher camps, followed by descents back to base camp. When they are ready, they will move beyond base camp to launch forays from camps higher on the mountain.

Pete's Adventure: THRILL SEEKERS

In 1996 Pete was at base camp preparing for his tenth trip up the mountain. One morning, the mood at base camp grew uneasy. Everyone watched as a pair of paragliders perched on a ledge near the Lho La. The pass is an area prone to rock slides and avalanches.

Pete figured the paragliders planned a horseshoe-shaped sweep over the camp and then a gentle landing. As the pair took off, he grew alarmed. The pilot was correctly harnessed into the glider. But his companion was not in the right position. She trailed beneath the pilot, attached by a 20-foot (6 m) rope. She kicked her legs clumsily, like a frail water bug. The people at base camp watched nervously as the pair floundered 1,000 feet (300 m) in the air, turned, and continued downward.

A paraglider sails through the skies above Everest.

Then the glider veered recklessly toward the treacherous Lho La. Within seconds, the pilot put the kite down on a small bank of hardened snow. But his partner slammed into a choppier snowbank near the base of the pass. The pilot hurried to unfasten himself. His partner lay motionless.

Working with several other experienced climbers, Pete quickly organized a high-altitude rescue. Retrieving the pair from the avalanche-prone pass would be dangerous. At any moment, the midday sun might melt the ice enough to loosen some rocks, sending them crashing down. Feeling like a human target, Pete remained alert and attentive. He carefully climbed up the pass with fellow climber ww. Finally, Pete and Todd reached the paragliders. The pilot was trying to aid the woman, who had a broken hip and a broken arm. She couldn't move and was in great pain.

Pete and Todd had carried metal backpack frames and foam sleeping pads up from below. They used the materials to make a crude stretcher. They carefully placed the woman inside. Cautiously and slowly, Pete and Todd maneuvered the device down the slope. They dodged falling rocks and ice. Meanwhile, the pilot moved swiftly down to base camp to help arrange rescue plans. As Pete and Todd neared base camp, other volunteer rescuers came up to assist them.

Afterword

At base camp, doctors gave the woman emergency first aid. They watched her for a day and a half. They also planned to evacuate her by helicopter. When the helicopter arrived, Pete directed the pilot's safe landing. He helped place the fragile woman inside the helicopter. The helicopter took the woman to Kathmandu for more medical treatment.

▲
A rescue helicopter speeds toward Mount Everest base camp.

ASK MR. EVEREST

How do you go to the bathroom on Mount Everest?

On Everest, many climbers pee into special bottles. They empty them at urine dumping sites on the mountain. The sites are marked with flags or stacks of rocks. It's important that people don't just pee in the snow, because climbers get their drinking water from melted snow. If the snow is contaminated, so is the drinking water.

Climbers collect solid waste in bags or cans, which they must cart off the mountain. Generally, high-altitude climbing tends to lessen the appetite. So climbers may not produce as much solid waste as normal. When climbers need to go, stripping off clothing on the mountain can be a hassle. Most climbers try to take care of their bathroom needs before they put on their gear in the morning.

Human waste isn't the only problem on Everest—trash is too. Cleanup efforts, like this one led by Nepali climbers in 2010, have removed tons of trash from the mountain.

CHAPTER 2

The Khumbu Icefall is an unimaginable place where unbelievable things sometimes happen.

—Mt. Everest

Towers of ice—some as tall as twelve-story buildings—invade the sky. They bulge, lean, and threaten to crash down at any instant. The frozen, cracked ground splits and disappears deep into darkness. The Khumbu Icefall is an unstable area, where the terrain can shift without warning. Climbers hope they are lucky on each journey through the icefall.

The Khumbu Icefall is a large glacier, or mass of moving ice, above base camp. It is the first big obstacle that climbers encounter on the trip up Everest. The walls of the icefall, called seracs, can tower 120 feet (37 m) high. Climbers must pass beneath them, clamber across them, and climb their steep faces. Seracs sometimes collapse, sending enormous blocks of ice crashing down. Their movement can also set off avalanches.

An Unsettling Crossing

Other challenges on the icefall are large holes called crevasses. Some are more than 100 feet (30 m) deep. To cross them, climbers use metal ladders lashed together to form bridges. It can take up to twelve ladders to reach across a single crevasse.

To help the climbers, Sherpas set up ladders on the icefall ahead of time. Sherpas also string ropes across crevasses and other sections of the icefall. The ropes are secured to the ice by devices called ice screws or snow pickets.

Climbers use clips called carabiners to attach themselves to the ropes. The carabiners connect to a person's climbing harness, which is worn around the waist and thighs. If a climber slips, the secured rope will catch him or her. To keep their footing on the icefall, climbers also wear crampons on the underside of their boots. These metal claws dig into the frozen ground.

▲ **Climbers rely on ladders to help them cross deep crevasses in the Khumbu Icefall.**

◄ **Parts of the icefall are covered with jagged chunks of ice.**

Pete's Adventure: ICE AVALANCHE!

By the time of his 1991 expedition, Pete had been through the Khumbu Icefall many times. But this time, he wondered if he would be unlucky. Several times, he had had the same nightmare. In the dream, he watched his backpack slowly fall into a bottomless crevasse. The dream set off uneasy thoughts.

On this trip through the icefall, Pete was with his good friend Lopsong Sherpa. Ahead of the other climbers in their group, they reached a series of three ladders that crossed a wide crevasse. As Pete clipped himself to a rope that ran alongside the ladders, he called playfully in Nepali to Lopsong. "Bad time to visit America," he said.

He knew Lopsong was familiar with the jest. It meant that a fall into a crevasse was like falling all the way through Earth, right to the other side, and coming out in America.

"Bad time," Lopsong chimed back.

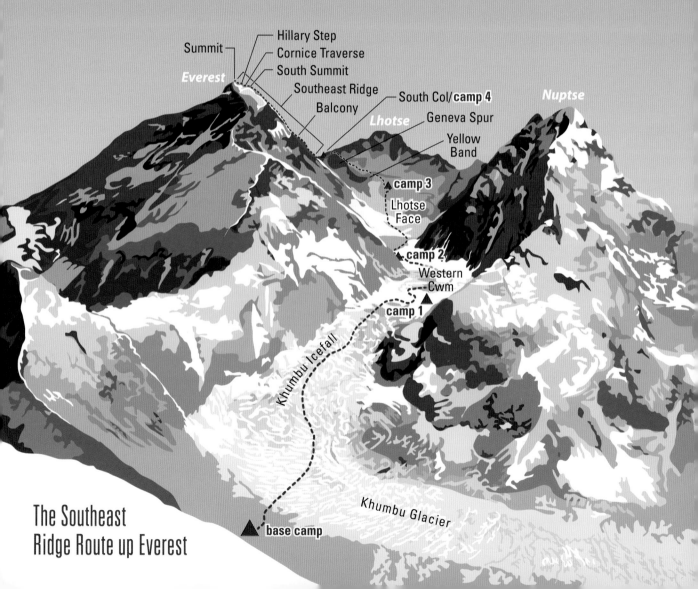

Hillary Step
Summit
Cornice Traverse
South Summit
Everest
Southeast Ridge
Balcony
South Col/camp 4
Lhotse
Geneva Spur
Nuptse
Yellow Band
camp 3
Lhotse Face
camp 2
Western Cwm
camp 1
Khumbu Icefall
Khumbu Glacier
base camp

The Southeast
Ridge Route up Everest

The Eight Thousanders

The Himalayan range is the only place on Earth with mountains above 8,000 meters (26,247 feet). There are fourteen "Eight Thousanders" in all.

RANGE	HEIGHT IN METERS	HEIGHT IN FEET
Everest	8,850	29,035
K2	8,611	28,251
Kanchenjunga	8,586	28,169
Lhotse	8,516	27,939
Makalu	8,481	27,825
Cho Oyu	8,201	26,906
Dhaulagiri	8,167	26,794
Manaslu	8,163	26,781
Nanga Parbat	8,125	26,656
Annapurna I	8,091	26,545
Gasherbrum I	8,068	26,470
Broad Peak	8,047	26,400
Gasherbrum II	8,035	26,361
Xixabangma Feng	8,027	26,335

Pete took his time stepping across the metal rungs. He placed each toe carefully.

"Almost there, Peter-Dai," he heard his friend call. *Dai* is the Nepali term for "older brother." Moments later, Pete stepped off the ladders and unfastened himself from the rope. Had his nightmare been just a bad dream after all?

As Pete watched Lopsong cross the ladders, a noise like an explosion rang out. A long, powerful *whoosh* and *crack* followed.

A climber makes his way through the Khumbu Icefall using ropes and wearing special ice climbing shoes.

Pete scanned the area. He knew that close by, a large serac had just collapsed. But before he could pinpoint the location, tremors surged through the frozen ground. Pete nearly lost his balance.

Pete struggled to steady himself. He glanced at his friend. Lopsong was clutching the edges of his wobbling ladders. Suddenly, a nearby serac started crumbling and falling apart. Huge sheaths of ice hurdled down. They crashed into one another and poured into the crevasse that Lopsong was crossing. A stray ice boulder shot out and toppled onto a section of the ladders, mangling them. The ladders fell into a river of ice below. Lopsong was left dangling from the ropes. He bobbed 1 foot (0.3 m) beneath the opening of the crevasse.

"Hang on!" Pete shouted. Pete didn't know if he should put himself in danger by trying to save Lopsong. Before he could decide, the crevasse began to open like giant jaws of a hungry shark. The ropes supporting Lopsong began to stretch, sending him farther down into the crevasse. Slabs of ice continued to churn down the choppy, steel-blue river below. Then Lopsong's ropes snapped. He fell out of sight. Pangs of terror ripped through Pete's heart.

Just when Pete was sure his friend had died, the ice river stopped flowing. The serac had become a mound of icy rubble. Pete dashed along the edge of the crevasse. He spied Lopsong a short distance away. He had fallen about 10 feet (3 m). He was buried waist-deep in chunks of ice.

"Not a good day to visit America," Lopsong said with a shaky voice. Pete chuckled as he lowered himself into the crevasse to free his friend from the ice.

Afterword

Pete, Lopsong, and all the other expedition members safely made it out of the icefall that day. But Lopsong's backpack was smashed and whisked away in the river of ice—much like the pack in Pete's dream. Meanwhile, the team was able to replace its equipment and continue up the mountain.

ASK MR. EVEREST

▶ What is a yeti, and have you ever seen one?

According to Himalayan stories, legends, and eyewitness accounts, a yeti is a creature resembling a large baboon. It supposedly has thick orange hair, a pointy head, long arms, short legs, and a long back. Most scientists say there's no such thing as a yeti. But many Sherpas, including Tenzing Norgay, claim to have seen them.

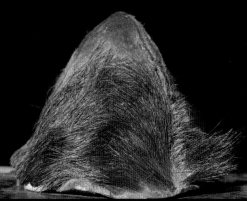

In all my years on Everest, I've never seen a yeti. But during several early trips to Everest, I saw what was said to be a yeti scalp *(right)*. It was encased in a glass container at a village monastery. It resembled a hairy half football. Skeptics, or disbelievers, think the "yeti scalp" was really the hide from a different kind of animal.

On Everest you can unexpectedly lose your life to something you'll rarely encounter on almost any other mountain on Earth: severe heat.

After the dangers of the Khumbu Icefall, camp 1 is a welcome sight for climbers. But most climbers don't stay long. If they are well acclimatized, they quickly move on to camp 2.

On the route from camp 1 to camp 2, climbers cross the Western Cwm (KOOM). In the Welsh language, *cwm* means "valley." The Western Cwm is also called the Valley of Silence because it's peaceful and quiet. The terrain has a gentle slope and is not too difficult to climb. Still, major crevasses run across the valley. Climbers avoid them by following a narrow passage known as Nuptse Corner.

The sun shines brightly on these climbers making their way across the Western Cwm.

Climbers begin their journey through the Western Cwm in the early morning. At this time, temperatures can be as low as –10°F (–23°C). But as the sun comes up and reflects off the snow and ice, temperatures can reach 90°F (32°C) or more.

To prepare for the Western Cwm, climbers often dress in easily removable layers of clothing. For protection against the sun's harmful ultraviolet rays, climbers cover their heads and necks with hats or scarves. They wear sunglasses or goggles to protect their eyes. They cover any exposed skin with sunscreen and put balm on their lips. Hazards such as dehydration, heat fatigue, and heat exhaustion are common. Some climbers get hyperthermia, or severe heat exhaustion. It can be fatal.

In addition to the extreme temperatures, climbers encounter thinner and thinner air. The higher they go, the less oxygen there is. Climbers struggle to breathe. They feel the effects of hypoxia, or oxygen deprivation. This condition makes them sluggish. Normally simple tasks such as removing a jacket or grabbing a water bottle can become difficult.

Camp 2 sits at 21,500 feet (6,550 m) above sea level. Climbers rest here before climbing farther up the mountain.

Back to Camp

Camp 2, at around 21,500 feet (6,550 m), resembles a small version of base camp. It has room for many climbing teams and large cook tents. The sun's heat melts snow and ice, forming lakes and streams. These give climbers water for washing and drinking.

Pete's Adventure: ESCAPE FROM THE DEADLY SUN

During Pete's 2002 expedition, Pete's team was moving through the Valley of Silence. He expected a slow climb. It was the group's first trip to camp 2. The thinning air challenged the climbers. The sun had been out for an hour, sending temperatures soaring. Team members had already stopped many times to shed extra clothes and to drink water.

Pete paused to rest. He gazed up at the tents at camp 2. They seemed close, but Pete knew the team had to endure another thirty minutes of sweltering heat before they would reach the tents. "It's like a mirage [an optical illusion]," he said to his climbing companion Brent Bishop.

"Yeah, we've got a ways to go still," Brent replied.

Brent moved on as Pete glanced back at climber Liesl Clark. She trailed 100 feet (30 m) below. She marched slowly, like a windup toy. Pete waved at her.

She returned a weak wave and resumed her slow journey. Detecting nothing out of the ordinary, Pete continued on.

In early afternoon, Pete finally reached camp. He greeted Brent, who had arrived only moments before. He happily accepted a cold drink offered by a Sherpa cook. But as Liesl approached the camp shortly afterward, Pete grew worried. He immediately noticed that her face was red. Her clothing hung limp with sweat.

"Hey, Liesl, are you well?" he asked.

"I'm just going to rest in the tent," she said.

Her breathing was strained. Pete hoped that a short rest would revive her.

Checking her condition shortly afterward, Pete found that she was burning with a 110°F (43°C) fever. "How are you feeling, Liesl? Are you feeling poorly?"

Liesl was conscious. But she did not respond to his questions. Based on these unmistakable signs, Pete knew she was very ill with hyperthermia. If he could not cool her down, she would be in serious trouble. She could die.

With Brent's help, Pete searched through the gear for scarves, rags, and other pieces of cloth. He soaked them in cool water from a mountain stream. He applied the wet cloths to Liesl's body as she rested in the tent. He hoped the water would cool her down. But after thirty minutes, she remained quiet and listless.

Pete wondered whether he and Brent should dunk Liesl in cold water. He figured they could rig a makeshift tub using materials from the cook tent and other gear. He knew this process would be risky. Liesl was already in a weakened state.

Hyperthermia— a Lesser-Known Mountain Illness

Many people have heard of hypothermia. This ailment occurs when the body gets too cold. It might be hard to believe amid all the snow and ice, but climbers on Everest can have the opposite problem. Heat cramps, heat exhaustion, and heatstroke can sicken and even kill climbers. These ailments are all forms of hyperthermia, an overheating of the body. Treating the most severe hyperthermia involves cooling the person down immediately. Otherwise, the body will begin to shut down. The person could die.

Medical Services on Everest

Most early expeditions to Mount Everest did not have an expedition doctor. Modern expeditions sometimes hire doctors to attend to sick climbers. In 2003 a group called the Himalayan Rescue Association (HRA) began a medical clinic at base camp. The clinic stays open from April 1 until the end of the spring climbing season in May. Staffed with paid medical professionals and volunteers, the HRA clinic treats anyone requiring medical care.

When climbers are up on the mountain, they can talk to doctors at base camp via radio. Some doctors even climb high on the mountain to assist sick climbers. Some go all the way to the summit if necessary. Doctors on Everest can consult with doctors in Kathmandu by satellite telephone.

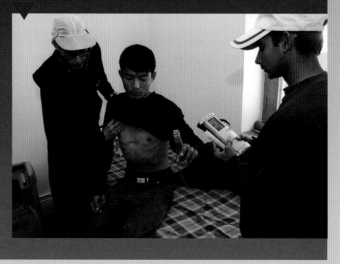

A climber who needs medical assistance gets treated at a clinic run by the Himalayan Rescue Association.

Most doctors on Mount Everest are familiar with high-altitude illnesses. Some expedition leaders, including Pete, have emergency medical training. They can recognize high-altitude sicknesses, aid ill climbers, and perform rescue operations.

She was dehydrated from the day's climb and hypoxic. Immersing Liesl in the icy 40°F (4°C) water could send her system into shock.

The situation did not look good. Pete wrestled with the options. He decided to continue with the wet cloths for fifteen more minutes. If she did not improve, he would then immerse her in water and hope for the best.

As the deadline neared, Liesl slowly seemed to improve. Her color looked better. She became responsive and aware.

"Liesl, are you well?"

"No, I'm feeling very, very bad," she replied.

These were pleasing words to Pete. It is a good thing to be aware of how bad off you are on Everest. Climbers who are really sick often don't have their wits about them. They might not even realize they are sick. They don't always ask for help when it is badly needed.

Afterword

Liesl made a full recovery. Although she did not reach the summit on that trip, she was able to go to higher camps on the mountain.

ASK Mr. EVEREST

How often do you shower and brush your teeth on Everest?

At base camp you can take a shower. Most expeditions set up a shower stall. Climbers or Sherpas heat water on a cookstove. They pour the water into a big bucket or bag on top of the stall. Inside, the person uses a hose to wash with hot water from above. Some people take sponge baths in their tents.

Above base camp, most people don't shower or wash their hair. But many continue to wash their hands using melted snow. Sometimes toothpaste tubes burst at high altitude. So many climbers brush their teeth without toothpaste.

What about shaving and haircuts?

Some male climbers don't shave on the mountain, but many do. I do, because my beard isn't thick enough to protect me from the sun. And when I have a scruffy beard, sunscreen doesn't stick to my face. Also, oxygen masks [used to help climbers breathe above camp 3] have a better seal on a freshly shaven face. I usually get a closely cropped haircut at Kathmandu. That lasts for the entire time I'm on Everest.

CHAPTER 4

Forged into Ice

On the less-traveled routes up Everest, you make tough decisions that you think will lessen your risks. That's the best you can do.

— Mt. Everest

Climbers attempting to summit Mount Everest can choose from up to eighteen different routes. Most climbers approach the mountain from the south, through Nepal, using the Southeast Ridge Route. Others approach from the north, through Tibet, using the Northeast Ridge Route. The West Ridge Route is a less popular route. It shares camps 1 and 2 with the Southeast Ridge Route. But then it goes its own way.

From camp 2, most climbers follow the Southeast Ridge Route. They make their way up the steep and slippery slope of the Lhotse Face. This is the western side of Lhotse, the fourth-highest peak in the Himalayas.

Climbers clip into a line of ropes that are secured into the mountain with metal anchors. Climbers move higher and higher using tools called ascenders. These tools slide up the ropes and lock in place. Climbers use ascenders as handholds.

The climb up the ropes can be slow. For one thing, climbers are sluggish in the thin air. They must rest often. Sometimes the ropes are crowded with climbers, so each person must wait his or her turn. Hypothermia and frostbite (freezing of the tissue of part of the body) are very real dangers as climbers linger in the subzero temperatures.

▲
This photo shows the Khumbu Icefall up to the Western Cwm. The peaks are Everest *(left)*, Lhotse *(center)*, and Nuptse *(right)*.

At 23,600 feet (7,200 m), camp 3 is nothing more than a cluster of two- and four-person tents perched on a ledge halfway up the Lhotse Face. Climbers often secure their tents to the ledge using ropes. The ropes also serve as handrails so climbers don't slide off the mountain.

Most climbers begin using bottled oxygen around camp 3. They breathe through masks connected to oxygen canisters. Although at this point the climbers are acclimatized to high altitude, the air above camp 3 is just too thin to breathe without help. Only extremely fit climbers sometimes choose not to use bottled oxygen above camp 3. Sherpas, who live at high altitude their entire lives and thus are very well acclimatized, often go without bottled oxygen.

The West Ridge Route to Camp 3W

The West Ridge Route up Everest is one of the most difficult. The route has been climbed successfully only six times since 1963. Twenty-three people have died trying. On much of the West Ridge Route, climbers rarely encounter other people.

Pete's Adventure: IN HARM'S WAY

Pete's 2002 expedition marked his second attempt to reach the summit of Everest via the dangerous West Ridge Route. He had tried in 1985, on his very first expedition to the mountain. But his oxygen equipment had malfunctioned. He had to turn back.

This second ascent up the West Ridge Route would be exhausting. But Pete was up for the challenge. The trip was also unfinished business since he had failed on his first attempt. It was unfinished business for his climbing partner Brent Bishop as well.

Climbers set up at camp 3. They've had to dig out a ledge in the snow to create a flat surface for their tents.

Pete *(left)* and other climbers head out of camp 3 and begin the steep climb up the South Col.

Brent's father, Barry Bishop, had tried unsuccessfully to climb the West Ridge Route in 1963.

On this expedition, Pete and Brent forged their way to a position about 2,400 feet (730 m) above camp 2. The terrain was steep and demanding. The climbers had to make a trail by chopping away snow and ice with ice axes. On top of this challenge, they had to set their own ropes. There were no fixed lines set ahead of time by Sherpas. Pete and Brent were the first climbers on the West Ridge Route that season.

"How's this spot?" asked Brent, coming to a rest. By then he had developed a steady cough. He struggled to breathe.

"It's not great, but we can dig in a tent platform," replied Pete. He scanned the area. "If we go higher, we'll risk bad acclimatization."

At 24,000 feet (7,315 m), the site Brent had chosen would be a suitable place. But it had one downside. This part of the West Ridge Route was a gully, or valley. Icy snow, jagged rocks, and small boulders ran down into the gully from higher points on the mountain.

"If we make camp to the side of the gully, it'll be the best spot of the bad spots," said Pete. "We won't be in a direct line of fire. But we may get debris [small rocks and pieces of ice]." He clipped his harness into a snow picket that he had hammered into the frozen ground. Then he drew his ice ax and began chopping a platform into the ice.

By nightfall Pete and Brent had secured their small tent snugly onto the side of the mountain. Pete then radioed his team at base camp. He said they had established camp 3W (or camp 3 west) and were settling in for the night.

Rest didn't come easy. Shortly after Pete made his call, the wind picked up and grew powerful. The tent walls heaved in and out. Pete and Brent sat up. They positioned their backs against the nylon walls of the tent. They grasped the metal ribs that supported the tent, trying to keep it from collapsing. The noise from the wind made conversation impossible.

If the weather remained just a windstorm, Pete and Brent had a good chance of riding it out. If it turned into heavy snow or a blizzard, all bets were off. Hearing no storm reports on the radio, Pete held onto the hope that conditions would improve. Then a loud rumble, like a freight train, cut through the wind.

From above, rocks began to pelt the tent. Pete feared that sharp rocks would slice the tent open. Had the ledge surrounding the tent been bigger, Pete was sure it would have been littered with piles of rock. Instead, the rubble made its way down the slope. Pete hoped it did not fall on those at camp 2.

The windstorm continued into the night and early morning. Finally, camp 3W quieted. It was time to move on. He and Brent needed to break trail and set lines for their higher camps. "Brent, we've gotta go," he said into the darkness. Brent stirred.

Pete was hoping the weather wouldn't destroy camp 3W before they were done using it. They would need to spend at least one more night there before they were fully acclimatized for their summit bid. After all, it was the best of the bad spots.

▲ **A fierce storm nearly buried these climbers at camp 3.**

Dress for Success on Mount Everest

Everest mountaineers need more than great skill. They must also have the right gear. The following list of essentials comes from climber Todd Burleson. He is the founder of Alpine Ascents International, a guiding company based in Seattle, Washington.

ASCENDERS: metal devices that slide up ropes and lock into place. Climbers use them as handholds.

CARABINERS: metal clips for fastening items together

CLIMBING BOOTS: heavy boots with plastic outer shells

CLIMBING HARNESS: a body harness used to secure a climber to a rope or an anchor point. Climbers also attach equipment to their harnesses.

CRAMPONS: spiked devices worn on the underside of climbing boots. They create traction (grip) on ice and snow.

GAITERS: protective coverings worn over boots and lower legs to seal out snow and ice

GLACIER GLASSES: sunglasses with side coverings to protect the eyes against sunlight and glare from the snow

HEADLAMP: a lamp that straps to the head to provide light in darkness

ICE AX: a pick that helps climbers grip snow and ice, carve footholds and tent platforms, break trails, and stop falls

TREKKING POLES: metal poles that climbers can lean on for support

Climbers also need warm down parkas, down pants, and other clothing. Miscellaneous necessities include sunscreen, lip balm, water bottles, toilet paper, and cooking gear.

Afterword

Eventually, jet stream winds kicked up a hostile storm. Pete and Brent had to abandon the West Ridge Route. They rejoined their expedition team on the Southeast Ridge Route. That team included Peter Hillary, son of Edmund Hillary. He, Pete, Brent, and other team members successfully reached the summit along the Southeast Ridge Route.

Pete, wearing crampons to keep from slipping on the ice, heads up the steep Lhotse Face.

ASK MR. EVEREST

Have there been any deaths on your expeditions?

We once lost a cook, Kami Sherpa. He fell from just above camp 3. He fell down the mountain and right past our team as we were going up to camp 3. It was a terrible loss.

How did this tragedy occur?

Kami Sherpa was about twenty-two years old. He worked as our cook at camp 2. He was very strong but not very experienced. Our *sirdar* (head Sherpa) sent him to the next camp with some more experienced Sherpas. Unfortunately, the men raced to see who could go fastest. Kami moved quickly to camp 4. He dropped his gear and then raced with the other Sherpas back down the ropes. He didn't clip in. He just held onto the ropes with his hands. He lost his footing and fell close to 2,500 feet (762 m) down the west face of Lhotse.

How did the young man's death affect the expedition?

It was very hard to proceed with the expedition. The Sherpa team was downhearted. We did not summit that year.

How do the Sherpas view the risks of working with climbers?

The Sherpas are trying to create other, safer job opportunities for themselves. Some are becoming pilots, doctors, park rangers, and politicians. But for those who can't afford extra education, mountaineering is the best and highest-paying work. A skilled climbing Sherpa can make $2,000 to $5,000 each year. This is good money in their community. A good sirdar can make double that. So the temptation to work on the mountain is great.

In the best conditions, novice [beginning] mountaineers can be guided to the top of Everest. In the worst conditions, the best mountaineers in the world can't get there.

CHAPTER 5

Reaching camp 4 is daunting. It sits in an area called the Death Zone. In the thinning air, people can't think clearly and may make mistakes. At 26,000 feet (8,000 m), the ability to meet tough challenges starts to fall apart. This is where the real suffering begins.

Moving upward from camp 3, climbers are painfully aware that they are approaching the Death Zone. The cold, dry air leaves some climbers gasping for breath. Others have uncontrollable coughing fits.

Some climbers linger on the ropes, doubled over in painful breathlessness. Because the air is so thin, many climbers begin breathing bottled oxygen through their masks.

The climb from camp 3 to camp 4 is also an unforgiving obstacle course. Climbers must make it through snow, ice, and rock. For the first part of the journey, climbers clip into ropes. They continue their slow ascent up Lhotse Face. Crampons and ice axes help them maneuver through the snow and ice. Next, they call upon their rock climbing skills to tackle a craggy cliff called the Yellow Band. They place their feet carefully on the rock, which might be partially covered in snow.

Crossing the top of the Lhotse Face, they then combat the Geneva Spur. This is a wall of sheer black rock. Here, some climbers remove their crampons and tread cautiously up the rock's natural steps. But most simply climb through the snow.

Climbers in the Death Zone approach the Yellow Band. This cliff is made up of yellowish rocks.

Camp 4, or high camp, sits in an area called the South Col. Thirty or more tents might be squeezed into the small area. Climbers will spend a few hours here, preparing their gear before their bid for the summit. The jet stream often roars through the camp, rattling the tents and threatening to blow them away in seconds.

Pete's Adventures: Rescue in the Death Zone

On their 1996 expedition, Pete and climbing partner Todd Burleson were positioned at camp 3 for their summit bid. Late at night, Pete's radio crackled. Base camp radioed that more than eighteen climbers were missing on the South Col. They included Rob Hall, Scott Fischer, and many of Pete's other longtime mountaineering friends.

It was four in the morning when Pete and Todd hooked into lines on the Lhotse Face to launch a rescue at camp 4. Pete could hear the winds thrashing the upper mountain. He began moving swiftly. He had climbed from camp 3 to camp 4 many times, yet never with such feelings of urgency.

Approaching camp 4 was like entering a nightmare. About twenty climbers from different expeditions sat in the wreckage of collapsed tents and wind-strewn equipment. They were weak and disoriented.

Climbers and tents at camp 4. Camp 4 sits at 26,000 feet (7,920 m) above sea level, just 3,000 feet (915 m) shy of the summit.

▼

"Let's get them off the South Col," Pete told Todd. He knew the climbers had been too high for too long. The tents would not provide adequate shelter if the storm rumbling across the summit suddenly got worse.

Pete began to assess each climber. Some suffered from snow blindness, caused by intense glare from the sun and snow. They were temporarily unable to see. Others were victims of frostbite. All had been without sleep, water, and oxygen for nearly two days. "Tashi, Paani garnos" (Please make water), Pete told the Sherpas. The Sherpas constructed a quick kitchen to melt ice for drinking water.

The hours passed quickly as Pete and Todd aided the climbers. They grouped them into small teams to descend to lower camps with Sherpa guides. Pete radioed expeditions stationed below. He alerted them to watch for the distressed climbers on their way down.

After helping a small team set off, Pete was surprised to see two Sherpas descending from the upper mountain. With short ropes, they were towing Makalu Gau, leader of a Chinese expedition. He lay in a sleeping bag on top of some foam mattresses. Pete quickly went to their aid. He helped place Makalu into a tattered tent. "He's exhausted, but we [took] him down after warming [his] frostbite and resting [him]," one of the Sherpas told Pete. "We know nothing about the others."

Pete was intent on searching for Rob, Scott, and the other missing climbers. Suddenly, Todd called out, "Pete, it's Beck!" Seaborn "Beck" Weathers, a climber from Rob's team, had suddenly staggered into camp. His face was black with frostbite. His right arm was frozen over his head. His hands were as white and lifeless as marble. A film of ice coated his face, neck, and arms.

Pete and others quickly helped Beck into a tent. They put him inside a sleeping bag lined with hot water bottles. Beck could not see or use his hands. How would they get him down the mountain? They would have to move slowly on the passes and through the icefall. Pete knew that of the climbers still left at camp 4, he and Todd were the only ones who could pull this off. He would have to cancel his plans to go higher on the mountain in search of the others.

A pair of Sherpas approached in the twilight. "Peter-Dai," one began. His voice shook. "We made it to the Southeast Ridge but were forced back by heavy winds." Pete listened, deeply saddened by the additional news.

Helicopter Rescue

For many years, helicopters couldn't fly above 14,850 feet (4,500 m) because their engines did not have enough power in the thin air. That's about 3,300 feet (1,000 m) below Everest's base camp. So climbers who were injured on a mountain had to be helped to a lower altitude before a helicopter rescue could take place.

Modern helicopters can fly to the highest Himalayan peaks. In 2010 Nepalese helicopter pilot Sabin Basnyat made a daring high-altitude rescue at almost 23,000 feet (7,000 m). He airlifted three Spanish climbers to safety from Nepal's Annapurna I. This was the highest air rescue ever made.

The Sherpas had found one of the climbers, and he was dead. Pete knew that any others who were still alive could not survive another night on the mountain. He also knew that Beck absolutely had to be taken down the mountain first thing in the morning.

By dawn the wind had died down. Pete put himself in front of Beck, with Todd directly behind. Slowly, the team descended the mountain. They moved through the steep passes, down the Geneva Spur, and to the Yellow Band. There, members of another expedition assisted with the rescue. Although reaching this point in the descent normally takes forty-five minutes, it took them more than three hours.

Afterword

Other climbers came to Beck's aid at camp 3 and took over the descent to camp 2. There, a dangerous helicopter rescue ensued. The pilot took Makalu Gau off the mountain first. The pilot then returned for Beck Weathers.

Makalu and Beck both survived. But they had parts of their limbs amputated due to frostbite. Eight other climbers died in the storm. Among them were some of the finest high-altitude mountaineers in the world.

A memorial commemorating the death of expert climber Scott Fischer is a reminder of the dangers of Everest.

ASK MR. EVEREST

How did you assist Beck Weathers down the mountain?

I was in front of Beck. His arms were draped over my shoulders. Todd held onto his climbing harness in back. The three of us walked slowly, one foot and then the next, stepping together. We took a break every few minutes. We used the fixed rope for all it was worth. It stretched and strained under our weight. Beck showed remarkable determination and balance. He moved efficiently, even though his hands could not grasp the rope.

How dangerous was this?

It was pretty dangerous. But I was working with a partner I trusted. Fortunately, Todd and I are pretty big guys. We could help Beck move along effectively. Also, Beck's feet were in good condition. When we got to the top of Geneva Spur and looked down, we saw people coming up to help us.

How was Beck's attitude?

He knew he was in bad condition—in terrible condition in a lot of ways. But his spirits were good. Throughout the trip, he remained alert and conscious. He concentrated very hard on getting the job done. He had almost no use of his hands. But at times, he'd try to hold the ropes in the crook of his elbow. He was extremely motivated.

What were your thoughts about the helicopter rescue?

A helicopter rescue at that altitude had never been achieved before. I wasn't sure it was going to work. When it did, I was excited. But I wasn't convinced the pilot would be able to come back after picking up Makalu Gau. It was a huge achievement for that pilot and his craft to do what he did. Everyone was remarkably relieved.

Beck Weathers after arriving in Kathmandu. Evidence of his severe frostbite and windburns is visible.

CHAPTER 6

I always did the best I could, but I was never afraid to turn people around if the situation warranted [called for it]. You aren't ever guaranteed a ticket to the top.

—Mr. Everest

The day a team launches a bid for the summit is a big deal. For weeks, climbers have pushed themselves to extremes. They have endured unimaginable discomfort and pain, hoping it will pay off. For some it will. Others won't be so lucky. Forty percent of all deaths on Everest occur above 26,000 feet (8,000 m).

At camp 4, climbers lie in their tents and glance often at their watches. They are eager to try to reach the summit. They restlessly listen to the sound of their own breath trapped inside their black oxygen masks—in and then out.

Ready, Set, Go!

At around eleven at night, Sherpas pass out hot tea in thermoses. Climbers put on layers of warm clothing, plus boots, crampons, climbing harnesses, oxygen equipment, headwear, headlamps, and protective eyewear. They prepare small backpacks with tools, snacks, and water bottles. The Sherpa support teams carry extra oxygen canisters.

Climbers must leave extremely early in the morning so they can reach the summit before noon. This is the set turnaround time. Even if they are very close, climbers who haven't reached the summit by noon must turn around and begin their descent to camp 4. If they do not, they are taking a great risk. They might get stranded near the summit in the dark.

Obstacles

At around one in the morning, the climbers set out. They begin by ascending the South Col on a fixed rope. They move cautiously and almost in slow motion—one sluggish step after another. After about five hours, they

At camp 4, climbers make their final preparations for the summit. In the past, climbers often left empty oxygen canisters on the ground, but climbers have become more careful about cleaning up their litter.

arrive on the Balcony. It is situated on the Southeast Ridge at 27,700 feet (8,400 m). Just as it sounds, the Balcony is an icy platform. Climbers often rest there.

A climber crosses the Geneva Spur to the South Col with the aid of ropes.

Continuing on toward the South Summit, climbers might have to walk through waist-deep, avalanche-prone snow. If conditions are not snowy, climbers instead walk up a series of massive stone steps. Up to two hours later, they arrive at the South Summit, at 28,700 feet (8,750 m). This is not the final summit. It is another, lower peak that lies to the south. The South Summit is a giant hump of icy snow piled on top of rocky steps. It is roughly the size of a small school bus.

The Cornice Traverse is the next frightening challenge. It is a 400-foot-long (122 m) ridge capped with ice. Climbers carefully cross its knife-sharp edge. One misstep can result in a 10,000-foot (3,000 m) plunge down the mountain's Kangshung

Climbers on the Balcony

Face or an 8,000-foot (2,500 m) dive down the Southwest Face. Climbers are sure to clip into the fixed lines to prevent such catastrophes.

The Hillary Step, at 28,750 feet (8,750), is a 40-foot (12 m) wall of snow, ice, and rock. Climbers line up to take their turn ascending this famous feature, named after Edmund Hillary. It is the final obstacle before the summit.

Pete's Adventure: TURNAROUND

On his 1995 expedition, Pete was leading a group of clients. These were people who had paid to be guided up the mountain. Snow soared in the wind at camp 4. Spirals of snow also encircled the upper mountain. Pete hoped the storm would settle down.

It was just after midnight. The Sherpas had already delivered tea to the restless climbers. "We're ready, Peter-Dai," the head sirdar called to Pete. He strained to be heard above the wind.

The Sherpa team had checked the equipment—ropes, anchors, and ice axes. They had also stored extra oxygen canisters in their backpacks. They adjusted their packs and moved swiftly out of sight. They would prepare the climbing route on the upper mountain for Pete's clients.

Everest Cuisine

Deciding what to eat on Everest is a serious matter. Climbers must eat foods high in calories to keep up with the physical demands of their activities. Rice, pasta, potatoes, vegetables, and eggs are all good energy sources. At base camp and camp 2, Sherpa cooks often prepare the food. Above base camp, climbers typically eat prepackaged and dried foods. They also rely on energy bars, cereal bars, candy, and other high-energy snacks.

A Sherpa prepares a meal for climbers on Everest.

To avoid dehydration, climbers must drink a lot of water. This can be a chore at high elevations. Climbers must collect ice and boil it over a camp stove to make drinking water. They must sometimes treat the water with chemical tablets or ultraviolet light. These treatments kill harmful organisms, making the water safe to drink.

Climbers wearing oxygen masks rest before attempting the ascent up the Hillary Step—the final stage of the Southeast Ridge Route.

By one o'clock in the morning, the climbers were ready. Although the snow had stopped, the wind blew strong. The climbers inched into the darkness. Step . . . breath . . . step . . . breath . . . rest. Their progress into the cold, thinning air was slow. Two hours passed and then another hour.

Pete monitored the team's pace, their distance from the summit, and the time they needed for a safe descent back to camp 4. He hoped his Sherpa team was making steady progress with the route.

The blustery conditions concealed the Sherpas' whereabouts. But as Pete surveyed the mountain once again, he spied a pair of faint headlamps coming toward him through the snowy fog. "Peter-Dai," a Sherpa began breathlessly, "we have snow—lots of snow!" He raised his hand to a position high above his heaving chest. He shook his head.

Above the South Col, the Sherpa team had hit massive snowdrifts. Snow covered the route and buried the ropes more than 4 feet (1.2 m) deep. Pete would have to help the Sherpas break trail. It was the only way a bid for the summit would still be possible.

Pete raised his ice ax and planted it firmly in a snowdrift. He tugged the snow to the side and pulled the rope out from under its snowy sheath. Again and again, he dug his ax into the snow. The Sherpas followed. They swept snow from the trail with their hands and packed it down with their feet. Pete's clients followed behind them.

As the climbers toiled through the snowy maze, they rested often and used much of their oxygen. Daylight arrived. Two more hours passed. The climbers were clearly exhausted. They moved like snails. Each step required multiple puffs of oxygen and a lengthy rest period. It was clear to Pete that the expedition team was spent.

The climbers had been at it for ten hours. Yet Pete figured they might be six hours away from the summit. At their present rate, they wouldn't reach the summit until three or four o'clock—long past the noon turnaround time. Worse still, they risked running out of oxygen. Their prospects didn't look good. Standing midway between the Balcony and the South Summit, Pete returned his ax to his belt. He made the decision to turn the team around.

Afterword

Although most of the clients agreed with Pete's decision, one requested that a Sherpa still take him to the summit. Pete would not agree. He knew the climbers were too exhausted, and he was unwilling to split the group.

ASK MR. EVEREST

How did you become interested in high-altitude mountaineering?

When I was seven years old, I found a book on my parents' bookshelf. It had photographs of 1952 Swiss expeditions to Everest. The pictures fascinated me. I also became excited by the polar explorers Ernest Shackleton and Robert Scott, who explored the Antarctic region; Matthew Henson and Robert Peary, who led the first expedition to the North Pole; and Roald Amundsen, the first person to reach the South Pole.

Although my interest developed when I was really young, my career as a climber was gradual. I didn't start off thinking I would summit Mount Everest seven times. I built up my rock climbing skills, then my ice climbing skills. Eventually I took up high-altitude climbing, which combined my two interests.

CHAPTER 7

Getting to the top was a five-year process. I learned how *not* to climb Everest on four expeditions.

—Mr. Everest

A Buddhist holy man once said that the summit of Mount Everest is no bigger than the tip of a finger. He meant that reaching the summit isn't important. It is the physical and the mental journey up the mountain that is most challenging and rewarding. Still, most summiteers feel a surge of accomplishment while standing on "top of the world."

On a clear day, views from the summit are spectacular. Some climbers claim they can actually see the curvature of Earth. And other giant peaks in the Himalayan range appear across the horizon like jagged teeth in the jaw of a fearsome beast.

Upon arriving at the summit, climbers often share a high five or a hearty hug with others from their expedition. They might take a photograph. They might call family and friends back home on a satellite telephone. In the past, many climbers left special items, such as small flags or bracelets, at the summit. But in keeping with the "leave no trace" ethic of environmental preservation, most climbers no longer leave items on top of the mountain. Sherpas who summit often say a prayer of thanks to Miyolangsangma, a goddess who is believed to live on the mountain.

Celebrations usually last a short time. Most climbers are keenly aware that they are only midway through their extreme adventure. Once they have climbed the mountain, they must get back down. This can take several days.

Although climbing down might seem easier than going up, most accidents on Everest actually happen during the descent. In fact, deaths are four times greater during descents than during ascents. Climbers must be cautious and safeguard against the health, weather, and terrain hazards they encountered on the way up.

Pete's Adventure: An Intense First Summit

The 1990 expedition was Pete's fifth trip to Everest. Violent weather, equipment failure, and plain old bad luck had defeated him before. Once again, he was ready to try for the summit.

Camp 4 was under attack by strong winds and heavy snow on the morning of April 28. Still, Pete's expedition team set off for the summit under the leadership of Glenn Porzak. Their goal was to climb higher—at least to the Balcony.

But conditions grew worse. The winds picked up and thrashed the snow. The rope, the route, and the thinning air quickly became cloaked in white. Positioned well below the Balcony, Pete and the others retreated to base camp. The snow continued to fall. The forecast remained grim. Hunkered in his tent, Pete hoped he'd have time for another summit bid.

Days later, good weather returned and gave the team a second try. As the climbers were well acclimatized, they moved to camp 3 in two days. The clear weather held, but the temperature dipped severely. Pete feared that cold might ruin his second go. He anxiously awaited Porzak's direction as the team rested at the Yellow Band.

Climbers tackle the Hillary Step on their way to the summit.

High-Altitude Illnesses

Dr. Peter Hackett, executive director of the Institute for Altitude Medicine in Telluride, Colorado, explains that climbers on Everest must guard against many high-altitude dangers. These include the following:

ACUTE MOUNTAIN SICKNESS (AMS): swelling of the brain. Symptoms include headaches, loss of appetite, vomiting, weakness, dizziness, fatigue, and difficulty sleeping. If left untreated, AMS can lead to HACE *(below)*.

HIGH-ALTITUDE CEREBRAL EDEMA (HACE): severe swelling of the brain. Symptoms include severe headaches, vomiting, confusion, clumsiness, seizures, and coma. If left untreated, HACE can lead to death.

HIGH-ALTITUDE PULMONARY EDEMA (HAPE): fluid collection in the lungs. Symptoms include severe shortness of breath, persistent cough, tightness of the chest, wheezing, and a fast heart rate. If left untreated, HAPE can lead to death.

Allowing the body to slowly adjust to high altitude is key in preventing these life-threatening illnesses. Climbers should also drink plenty of liquids. If a climber does get sick, he or she should immediately descend to lower altitudes, rest, and breathe extra oxygen from canisters.

High altitude can also cause these less serious but uncomfortable complications:

ALTITUDE FLATUS EXPULSION: high-altitude farting, caused by a buildup of gas in the abdomen

CHEYNE-STOKES RESPIRATION: irregular breathing during sleep (four large breaths followed by a twelve-second lag in breathing)

CHRONIC MOUNTAIN SICKNESS: headaches, muscle aches, and difficulty with memory and concentration, caused by living at high altitude for many months

HIGH-ALTITUDE SYNCOPE: fainting

HIGH-ALTITUDE PERIPHERAL EDEMA: swelling of the arms, hands, legs, feet, and face

"This is it. Our shot. We're going for it!" Porzak said. Relieved by the words, Pete forged ahead into the cold thin, air toward camp 4.

Into the moonlight of May 9, Pete and the others set out from camp 4 toward the summit. Despite the freezing temperatures, their ascent was flawless. Then, high above the Balcony, Pete's oxygen equipment failed—just as it had on his 1985 expedition. He knew he had to make a critical decision: either retreat or take his chances without oxygen. Without oxygen, he might become disoriented and make poor decisions, putting his life in danger. A lack of oxygen could even lead to permanent brain damage.

Pete poses for a photo at the summit.

A team of climbers celebrates in 2010 after reaching the summit.

But this time, there would be no retreat. He forged ahead into the deep snow, well ahead of the others. He pushed onto the South Summit and across the Cornice Traverse.

A pile of jumbled rock encased in ice and snow blocked Pete's path to the summit. The safety rope was also completely concealed by ice and snow. He would have to dig it out as he inched his way up. Any fall could be fatal. With no partner nearby to help him, he could not afford a single mistake.

Pete was less than an hour from the summit when, almost majestically, the sun appeared. It cast brilliant rays across the horizon. Pete could feel the warmth hit the top of his head and trail down his shoulders. All at once, everything felt right. He continued the climb alone—all the way to the top of the world!

At last, he gazed with awe at the sight he had tried so many times to see. At last, he sensed accomplishment.

Afterword

Pete spent a few minutes on the summit before beginning his descent. Although he was well acclimatized, he started to feel very cold. He knew he had reached his physical limits and should get down quickly. Seven others from the expedition reached the summit later that morning.

ASK MR. EVEREST

Will you try for another summit on Everest?

I'm uncertain if I could top the experiences I've had on my other successful summits. In addition, it's almost unthinkable to consider taking the time away from my family to make another summit. I even entered a friendly pact with some of my close climbing buddies: if any one of us considers going back to Everest, the others will try and talk him out of it. But that pact's been broken a couple of times already.

Tens of thousands of visitors—climbers, trekkers, paragliders, and other thrill seekers—come to Everest every year. And the number of climbers and other visitors is growing. In the year 2000, fewer than fifty expedition teams tried to tackle the mountain. In ten years, by 2010, the number of expedition teams had more than doubled.

Climbing Everest has also become a more and more high-tech endeavor. Climbing equipment is stronger and lighter than ever before. Clothing is warmer. Helicopters can make higher and higher rescues when climbers get in trouble. In addition, "communication has improved significantly," explains Todd Burleson. "Today, up to five different companies provide weather forecasts for the mountain. Also, climbers have multiple ways to communicate—radio phones, beepers, live video, and e-mail."

Keeping Everest Clean

A downside to all the visitors to Everest is that they can make a mess of the mountain. They leave behind empty oxygen tanks, broken equipment, and other kinds of trash.

To keep the mountain clean, climbers have started several programs. For example, all climbing expeditions must pay a $4,000 garbage security deposit to the Nepalese Ministry of Culture, Tourism, and Civil Aviation. If climbers don't remove their garbage from the mountain, they lose the money. In addition, cleanup teams have collected tons of garbage from the mountain. In 2010, for example, the Extreme Everest Expedition, a team of Nepali climbers, led a massive cleanup effort near the Death Zone. They removed more than 2 tons (1.8 metric tons) of litter.

Is Everest in Your Future?

For kids who want to climb Everest or other mountains someday, Pete suggests starting with basic hiking and working up from there. Once you have some outdoor skills, you can take climbing classes.

A lot of organizations and gyms have rock climbing walls, where you can take lessons to develop your skills. Pete attended summer programs with the National Outdoor Leadership School and Outward Bound, which taught him advanced climbing techniques.

What's in Everest's Future?

According to Pete, Everest will continue to attract world-class mountaineers. Some teams will take on the challenge of blazing new routes up the mountain. Other climbers will test their skill on extremely difficult routes to the summit. Still others will set goals of summiting multiple peaks in a single expedition—for instance, climbing Everest and the neighboring Himalayan giants Lhotse and Nuptse all in one trip.

And of course, Everest will continue to attract thrill seekers, daredevils, and adventurers. New records will take the place of old ones. "With every season, there is some new record broken—the youngest climber, the oldest climber, the fastest ascent," says Pete. "It's a tradition on Everest. One that we'll continue to see time and time again."

Pete established the Nepal Magic Yeti Library in 2007. This organization gives books to Himalayan children and helps Himalayan villagers manage libraries.

1841 British surveyor George Everest records the location of a high Himalayan peak. Tibetans call the mountain Chomolungma. Nepalese call it Sagarmatha.

1852 British scientists determine that Chomolungma/Sagarmatha is the highest peak on Earth.

1865 Great Britain names the mountain in honor of George Everest.

1953 New Zealander Edmund Hillary and Sherpa Tenzing Norgay become the first climbers to reach the summit of Everest.

1963 Climbers make the first successful summit of Everest via the West Ridge Route.

1985 Pete Athans makes his first attempt to climb Mount Everest. He takes the West Ridge Route but fails at 28,100 feet (8565 m).

1990 Pete Athans reaches the summit of Everest on his fifth attempt to climb the mountain.

1996 Eight climbers die during a massive snowstorm on Everest.

1997 Journalist Jon Krakauer chronicles the 1996 disaster on Everest in his best-selling book *Into Thin Air.*

2003 The Himalayan Rescue Association establishes a medical clinic at base camp.

2007 Pete Athans, Liesl Clark, and other climbers establish the Nepal Magic Yeti Library to provide books to Nepalese children.

2010 The Extreme Everest Expedition removes more than 2 tons (1.8 metric tons) of litter from Mount Everest.

2011 Nepalese officials launch a two-year study to obtain an accurate measurement of the height of Mount Everest.

Glossary

acclimatize: to adjust to a new temperature, altitude, climate, environment, or other situation

altitude: height above sea level

ascend: to climb up

ascenders: metal devices that slide up ropes and lock into place. Climbers use them as handholds and to secure their safety harnesses to fixed ropes.

avalanche: a mass of snow, ice, and sometimes rock that forcefully slides down a mountain

balaclava: a knit cap that covers the entire head and neck, except for the wearer's eyes and nose

crampons: spiked devices worn on the underside of climbing boots to create traction (grip) on ice and snow

crevasse: a deep crack in the ground or in a glacier

dehydration: not having enough water inside one's body

descend: to climb down

elevation: height above sea level; altitude

evacuation: removing people from an unsafe place or situation

fixed ropes: ropes secured on a mountain route before climbers arrive. Climbers attach themselves to the ropes for safety.

forays: short climbs up and down sections of a mountain to help climbers acclimatize to high altitude

frostbite: freezing of the tissue of part of the body, such as fingers, toes, or ears

glacier: a large body of ice moving slowly down a slope or a valley

hyperthermia: an overheating of the body

hypothermia: a below normal body temperature

hypoxia: oxygen deficiency

ice ax: a tool used for digging into and gripping ice and snow

icefall: part of a glacier that has broken into jagged blocks of ice

ice screw: a metal spike screwed into ice to anchor a rope

jet stream: a band of fast-moving air currents flowing around Earth at high altitudes

porter: a person who transports materials, equipment, and other loads

rockfall: a mass of falling or fallen rocks

sea level: the average level of the surface of the ocean, used as a starting point for measuring the height of land formations

seracs: large blocks or towers of ice that make up an icefall

Sherpas: an ethnic group living in the Himalayan Mountains, mainly in northeast Nepal. Many Sherpas work as guides and assistants for Everest expeditions.

sirdar: the head Sherpa of a climbing expedition

snow blindness: temporary blindness caused by bright sunlight reflecting off snow and ice

summit: the top of a mountain. *To summit* means "to reach the top of a mountain."

Source Notes

9   Jon Krakauer, *Into Thin Air: A Personal Account of the Mount Everest Disaster* (New York: Villard, 1997), 7.

10 Pete Athans, telephone interview with author, April 16, 2006.

17 Pete Athans, telephone interview with author, May 27, 2008.

18 Pete Athans, interview with author, December 23, 2010.

23 Pete Athans, telephone interview with author, May 14, 2006.

23 Athans, interview, May 27, 2008.

24 Pete Athans, telephone interview with author, July 12, 2010.

28 Ibid.

29 Athans, interview, May 27, 2008.

30 Pete Athans, telephone interview with author, July 7, 2010.

34 Pete Athans, telephone interview with author, September 1, 2010.

37 Athans, interview, May 27, 2008.

38 Athans, interview, April 16, 2006.

41 Athans, interview, September 1, 2010.

43 Athans, interview, May 27, 2008.

44 Pete Athans, interview with author, October 25, 2010.

49 Athans, interview, May 27, 2008.

50 Athans, interview, April 16, 2006 .

54 Athans, interview, July 7, 2010.

55 Athans, interview, May 27, 2008.

56 Todd Burleson, telephone interview with author, February 2, 2011.

57 Pete Athans, telephone interview with author, October 27, 2011.

Selected Bibliography

Alpine Ascents International. 2011. http://www.alpineascents.com (August 27, 2011).

Coburn, Broughton. *Everest: Mountain without Mercy*. Washington, DC: National Geographic Society, 1997.

Everest: 50 Years on the Mountain. DVD. Washington, DC: National Geographic Video, 2003.

Hawley, E. *The Himalayan Database: The Expedition Archives of Elizabeth Hawley*. Rev. ed. Golden, CO: American Alpine Club Press, 2010.

Himalayan Experience. 2011. http://www.himalayanexperience.com (August 27, 2011).

Himalayan Rescue Association. N.d. http://www.himalayanrescue.org (August 27, 2011).

How the Earth Was Made: Everest. DVD. New York: A&E Television Networks, 2009.

Institute for Altitude Medicine. 2011. http://www.altitudemedicine.org (August 27, 2011).

Krakauer, Jon. *Into Thin Air: A Personal Account of the Mount Everest Disaster*. New York: Villard, 1997.

Unsworth, W. *Everest: The Mountaineering History*. 3rd ed. Seattle: Mountaineers, 2000.

Weathers, Beck. *Left for Dead: My Journey Home from Everest*. New York: Dell, 2000.

Further Reading

Books

Blanc, Katherine, and Jordan Romero. *The Boy Who Conquered Everest: The Jordan Romero Story.* Carlsbad, CA: Hay House, 2010.
This book tells the story of teenager Jordan Romero, the youngest person to climb all Seven Summits—the highest mountains on each of the seven continents.

Burleigh, Robert. *Tiger of the Snows: Tenzing Norgay: The Boy Whose Dream Was Everest.* New York: Atheneum, 2006.
This picture book introduces Sherpa Tenzing Norgay. In 1953 he and Edmund Hillary became the first people to reach the top of Mount Everest.

Chester, Jonathan. *Young Adventurers' Guide to Everest: From Avalanche to Zopkio.* Berkeley, CA: Tricycle Press, 2005.
This book presents a variety of information on Mount Everest. Readers can reference key words and phrases organized alphabetically.

Jenkins, Steve. *The Top of the World: Climbing Mount Everest.* Boston: Sandpiper, 2002.
This unique children's book offers historical information about Everest expeditions using cut-paper collage illustrations.

Korman, Gordon. *The Contest.* New York: Scholastic Book Clubs, 2008. This is the first of a series of three books, including *The Climb* and *The Summit,* which feature fictionalized stories of children who climb Mount Everest.

Taylor-Butler, Christine. *Sacred Mountain: Everest.* New York: Lee & Low Books, 2009.
This title presents an account of Mount Everest from the perspective of the Sherpa residents.

Venables, Stephen. *To The Top: The Story of Everest.* New York: Walker Books, 2004.
This book for young readers contains in-depth historical information on Everest and describes the author's 1988 expedition.

Werther, Scott P. *Jon Krakauer's Adventure on Mount Everest.* Danbury, CT: Scholastic Children's Press, 2002. Based on Jon Krakauer's *Into Thin Air,* this book tells the story of the 1996 disaster on Everest for young readers.

Websites

Experience Everest: The Razor's Edge
http://dsc.discovery.com/everesttheexperience/interactive/interactive.html
This interactive game allows you to join a virtual Everest expedition and test your skill in overcoming challenges to reach the summit.

I Was the First to Conquer Everest
http://www.teacher.scholastic.com/activities/hillary/
This website provides information about Edmund Hillary and Tenzing Norgay, the first climbers to summit Mount Everest.

Jordan Romero.com
http://www.jordanromero.com
Jordan Romero, the youngest Everest summiteer, shares his adventures on the world's seven summits and encourages viewers to find their own Everest.

Mount Everest Facts
http://kidzcoolzone.com/mount-everest-facts/
Discover historical facts about Mount Everest, and see what it's like to visit the Khumbu region. The website includes a narrated video and a 360-degree panoramic view of the mountain.

Quiz Your Noodle: Mount Everest
http://kids.nationalgeographic.com/kids/games/geographygames/quizyournoodle-mount-everest/
Test your knowledge about Mount Everest by taking an interactive quiz on this website. Also included is a link to a site featuring information about the Sherpas.

Relive the Experience: Climbing Everest
http://dsc.discovery.com/convergence/everest/everest.html
This site features a blog, Sherpa cams, and other details from some of the Discovery Channel's Everest expeditions.

LERNER SOURCE

Expand learning beyond this printed book. Download free, complementary educational resources for this book from our website, www.lernerresource.com.

Index

About the Author

Sandra K. Athans grew up watching her brother Pete turn his rock climbing hobby into a mountain climbing career. In addition to following his adventures, she teaches fourth grade and writes for children and teachers. She lives with her husband, two children, and three pets in Chittenango, New York.

photo courtesy of Claire Charde

photo courtesy of Pete Athans

Sandra Athans

Pete Athans

Photo Acknowledgments

The images in this book are used with the permission of: © Peter Barritt/Alamy, pp. 2–3; Courtesy of Pete Athans, pp. 4, 8, 26, 33, 36, 38–39, 44–45, 46 (both), 54 (top), 57; © Dan Rafla/Aurora/Getty Images, pp. 4–5; Rue Des Archives/The Granger Collection, New York, p. 6; © James Burke/Time & Life Pictures/Getty Images, p. 6 (inset); © Laura Westlund/Independent Picture Service, pp. 7, 20; © Galen Rowell/CORBIS, pp. 9, 32, 34; © Kulraj Bhogal/Alamy, pp. 10–11; © Dave Stamboulis/Alamy, p. 12 (top); © Christine Pemberton/The Image Works, p. 12 (bottom); © RM Nunes Photography/Flickr/Getty Images, p. 14; © Gamma-Keystone/Getty Images, p. 15; © Science Faction/SuperStock, p. 16; © Namgyal Sherpa/AFP/Getty Images, p. 17; © Michael Mellinger/Flickr/Getty Images, p. 18; © Doug Allan/NPL/Minden Pictures, p. 19; © Michael Brown/Serac Adventure Films/ZUMA Press, p. 22; © Hemis/Alamy, p. 23; © Aurora Photos/Alamy, pp. 24–25; © John Van Hasselt/CORBIS, p. 28; © Nicholas DeVore/Stone/Getty Images, pp. 30–31; © David Trood/Stone+/Getty Images, p. 35; © imagebroker.net/SuperStock, p. 40; © Design Pics/Philippe Wilding/Perspectives/Getty Images, p. 42; AP Photo/Binod Joshi, p. 43; © Jake Norton/Aurora Open/SuperStock, p. 47; © AFP/Getty Images, pp. 48, 52; © Stefen Chow/Aurora Photos/CORBIS, pp. 50–51; AP Photo/Team Romero, p. 54 (bottom).

Front cover: Todd Burleson, Alpine Ascents Collection.